Bright
≡Summaries.com

To the Lighthouse

BY VIRGINIA WOOLF

BOOK ANALYSIS

By Alba Díez de Ure

To the Lighthouse
BY VIRGINIA WOOLF

Bright
≡Summaries.com

VIRGINIA WOOLF

ENGLISH NOVELIST AND ESSAYIST

- **Born in London in 1882.**
- **Died in Rodmell (United Kingdom) in 1941.**
- **Notable works:**
  - *Mrs. Dalloway* (1925), novel
  - *Orlando* (1928), novel
  - *A Room of One's Own* (1929), essay

Virginia Woolf was one of the most important modernist authors of the 20th century and a pioneer in the use of many experimental prose devices. She was part of the Bloomsbury group, an artistic and literary group of intellectuals and bohemians who shared ideas about philosophy and the arts and rejected traditional habits. Woolf was also a prominent women's rights advocate and the founder of the Hogarth Press, through which she published most of her works.

During her literary career, her prose continuously evolved towards more experimental storytelling and narrative devices. For instance, she was a trailblazer in the use of the stream of consciousness technique (a literary device that strives to capture the multitude of thoughts that pass through a character's mind as part of a non-linear narrative).

Her life and work were affected by her sporadic mental breakdowns: she was institutionalised and attempted suicide on multiple occasions during her lifetime. At the age of 59, having fallen into another bout of depression and feeling anxious about the onset of World War II, she drowned herself in the river Ouse, near Monk's House, her home in Sussex (United Kingdom).

TO THE LIGHTHOUSE

AN EVOCATION OF FAMILY HOLIDAYS

- **Genre:** novel
- **Reference edition:** Woolf, V. (1993) *To the Lighthouse*. London: Longman Group Limited.
- **1st edition:** 1927
- **Themes:** the passage of time, memory, human and family relations, the subjectivity of life and experience, art and beauty as cures, war

To the Lighthouse tells the story of the Ramsay family and their holidays, focusing on just two days separated by ten years. Part One covers one day in the life of the members of the family and some of their acquaintances, who are staying on the Isle of Skye in Scotland. In Part Two, ten years go by, conveyed by the description of the now-abandoned holiday home. In Part Three, which is set ten years later, the remaining members of the family return to the holiday home and the adjacent lighthouse.

Woolf used the writing of this book to reflect on her memories of her own family and their holidays in the Hebrides off the coast of Scotland.

To the Lighthouse is one of the most important modernist novels of the 20th century. It was Woolf's fourth novel and the one that consolidated her position as a key writer at the time.

In *To the Lighthouse*, the plot and action are secondary to the philosophical and psychological examination of the characters' minds. The book uses the shifting point of view of different narrators to drive the story forward.

SUMMARY

The book follows the Ramsay family's holidays on two days separated by ten years. It is divided into three sections.

"THE WINDOW": A FAMILY AND THEIR HOLIDAYS

The Ramsays (Mr. and Mrs. Ramsay and their eight children) are spending their holidays at their summer home on the Isle of Skye, shortly before the outbreak of World War I. James, the youngest son, expresses his desire to go to the nearby lighthouse on a family excursion the next day. Mrs. Ramsay agrees but Mr. Ramsay, who is a philosopher and a strict father, dismisses the idea. This fills James with anger towards his father and leaves Mrs. Ramsay with doubts about their marriage.

The Ramsays are met at their holiday home by some friends, including Charles Tansley (Mr. Ramsay's young disciple and admirer) and the young painter Lily Briscoe.

During the day, a number of events happen: the children play cricket in the garden; Mrs. Ramsay sits by the window, knitting a stocking for the lighthouse keeper's son; and Mrs. Ramsay then invites Charles Tansley on a walk into town, where she tells him about Augustus Carmichael, another guest at the house. Carmichael is an opium user and poet whose work has not been successful yet.

Later, in the garden, Lily Briscoe begins painting Mrs. Ramsay by looking at her through the window. Mrs. Ramsay wants Lily Briscoe to marry William Bankes, a much older widower and another family acquaintance at the summer home. In the garden a sincere friendship begins to develop between them.

Meanwhile, Paul Raley and Minta Doyle, two other young guests in the family home, go for a walk on the beach together. Nancy, one of the daughters of the Ramsay family, goes with them. They are encouraged to do so by Mrs. Ramsay, who wishes Paul and Minta to marry. During the walk, Minta losses her grandmother's brooch and Paul proposes to her.

At night, everybody meets for dinner, but a number of incidents threaten to ruin the night: Paul Raley and Minta Doyle arrive late from their beach walk; Mr. Ramsay feels irritated when Mr. Carmichael asks for another plate of soup; and the Ramsay children laugh at their own inside jokes about the adults. However, the evening ends on a high note as the boeuf en daube (the main course) is exquisite.

Dinner ends and everybody goes to bed. James and Cam (two of the youngest Ramsay children) are intimidated by the boar's skull hanging on the wall of their bedroom. In the intimacy of their room, Mr. Ramsay and Mrs. Ramsay reassure one another of their love for each other.

"TIME PASSES": AN ABANDONED HOME

This section of the book navigates a ten-year span through the description of the now-abandoned family summer home. It starts when everybody at the summer home turns off their lamps to go to sleep. Darkness, the wind and other natural elements take over the house over the course of a decade. Three characters pass away during this period: Mrs. Ramsay dies unexpectedly one night; World War I breaks out and Andrew Ramsay (the oldest of the Ramsays' children) dies in battle; and Prue Ramsay (the oldest of the Ramsay's daughters) marries happily but then dies during childbirth. Meanwhile, Augustus Carmichael publishes his poetry to great success.

The summer home remains neglected and derelict for many years. After ten years have gone by, the remaining members of the family return to the house. Mrs. McNab, the housekeeper, cleans the house to restore it to its former glory.

Lily Briscoe and Augustus Carmichael arrive at the summer home, where they meet the remaining members of the Ramsay family, and everybody goes to bed.

"THE LIGHTHOUSE": HEALING PAST WOUNDS

In the morning, Mr. Ramsay decides that he, James and Cam will visit the lighthouse that day. James and Cam, who are now 16 and 17 respectively, are unenthusiastic about their father's, as they can see that he is continuing in his tyranni-cal ways.

In the garden and joined by a sleepy Mr. Carmichael, Lily Briscoe attempts to continue the painting she started the last time she visited the house, the one that depicted Mrs. Ramsay through a window. Her doubts about her artistic ability continue. While she is painting, Lily often looks out to the sea and sees the sailboat in which Mr. Ramsay, James and Cam are going to the lighthouse.

In the boat, Mr. Ramsay is behaving anxiously in an attempt to attract sympathy and love from his children. However, James and Cam secretly decide to continue the journey in silence as a way of punishing their father for his selfishness. Soon, Cam caves to her father's needs and stops behaving indifferently towards him.

James reflects on how the lighthouse was an unattainable dream when he was a child and how, now that he is about to visit it, it seems less attractive. When he looks at his father reading, he sees him as a sad, old man and recognises how both he and his father feel lonely. When his father praises him upon arriving at the lighthouse, James changes his attitude and feels affectionate towards him.

Back in the summer home's garden, Lily is overwhelmed by her memories of Mrs. Ramsay. She also reflects on how Minta and Paul's marriage was with time revealed to be an unhappy one. Unbothered by other people and drawing upon her sympathetic feelings for Mrs. Ramsay, Lily is finally able to overcome her doubts and complete the painting.

CHARACTER STUDY

MRS. RAMSAY

Mrs. Ramsay is an "astonishingly beautiful" woman (p. 108), a loving mother of eight and a very supportive wife, and many of the other characters are fond of her (her husband and her youngest son James love her; Charles Tansley falls in love with her; Lily Briscoe admires her).

Mrs. Ramsay embodies Woolf's idea of a woman content with traditional gender roles. She enjoys giving special attention to men and feels sympathetic towards what she considers their fragile egos. She is also happy with her role as a hostess and works hard to make everyone happy during their stay at the Ramsays' summer home.

She enjoys influencing people into doing what she believes is right. For instance, she acts as a matchmaker for some characters, with varying degrees of success (Minta and Paul, Lily and William). Lily's indifference towards marriage leaves Mrs. Ramsay confused. However, she still respects her.

Mrs. Ramsay herself struggles with her own marriage. She is concerned about her husband's changing moods, but she believes it is her role as a wife to constantly alleviate his insecurities about his career.

Although she is satisfied by her role in the family, her inner thoughts show that she is sometimes melancholic. She is especially preoccupied with the passage of time, particularly when it comes to her children growing up.

Mrs. Ramsay is at the centre of her family's life. When she dies, the Ramsays go through a very dark decade. Her character is loosely based on Woolf's mother.

MR. RAMSAY

Mr. Ramsay is a metaphysical philosopher and a reputable intellectual among his peers. He is presented as a serious academic, who often quotes the masters of literature and who is highly respected by his disciples, including Charles Tansley.

As a family man, he is different: his children see him as selfish, tyrannical and extremely severe.

Furthermore, his relationship to women is ambivalent: he believes women are irrational but needs them in his life for constant reassurance. He is insecure about the value of his work and constantly thinks about the fate of his writing after he dies.

During the first part of the book, he turns to Mrs. Ramsay for sympathy whenever he feels insecure. After Mrs. Ramsay dies, he seems lost and seeks sympathy in Lily Briscoe (another female figure) and his children (especially James and Cam during the trip to the lighthouse).

Mr. Ramsay's character is loosely based on Woolf's own father.

LILY BRISCOE

Lily Briscoe embodies Woolf's many concerns with art and women's roles in society.

First and foremost, she represents Woolf's own doubts and hesitancy about her artistic practice. Over the course of the ten-year span, Lily evolves from a beginner artist who struggles to put her vision to the canvas to someone who learns to trust her own ideas and artistic decisions. This evolution is analogous to Woolf's.

Lily has got "little Chinese eyes" (p. 13). She is revealed to be an independent woman, and not one particularly interested in marriage. In fact, she and William Bankes become good friends, despite Mrs. Ramsay's insistence that they should marry.

Likewise, the novel also discusses Lily's role as a female artist and the way that this is perceived by society (again an exploration of Virginia Woolf's own experience). This is exemplified through three different episodes in which men judge her art. First, Charles Tansley's comments that women cannot paint or write repeatedly echo in Lily's ears throughout the novel. Second, Lily is afraid that Mr. Ramsay will look at her painting at the beginning of the book and, by the end, it is only when Mr. Ramsay finally leaves that she can finish her painting. On the contrary, the interest that William Bankes pays to her painting strengthens her artistic vision.

JAMES RAMSAY

James is the Ramsays' youngest child. He feels a profound love for his mother and a deep loathing for his father. In the first part of the novel, James hates his father for not allowing him to go to the lighthouse, and has murderous thoughts towards him. He sees his father as a selfish tyrant, and is envious of his father's relationship with Mrs. Ramsay.

In the third part of the novel, Mrs. Ramsay's death leaves father and son alone to resolve their conflict. Although he still sees his father as a despot, James shifts his perspective on the journey to the lighthouse and finally perceives the profound loneliness both he and his father feel. He is able to notice many of his father's characteristics in himself, including the need for reassurance.

CHARLES TANSLEY

Charles Tansley is Mr. Ramsay's pupil. He is obsessed with his reputation and believes only Mr. Ramsay can equal his intellect at the summer home. Moreover, he believes women to be intellectually inferior to men. None of the guests are fond of him, and the children frequently mock him, calling him "atheist" (p. 3).

It is revealed on his walk into town with Mrs. Ramsay that he is extremely insecure because of his humble, working-class background. During this walk, he falls in love with Mrs. Ramsay's charm, beauty and kind reassurance.

ANALYSIS

MODERNISM AND EXPERIMENTATION

Modernism is a literary, artistic and philosophical movement that emerged in the early 20th century. This movement is characterised by the rejection of tradition on the grounds that it is obsolete and the search for innovation to create a new form of art.

Modernism developed as a reaction to major changes in society: the philosophical, scientific and technological revolutions and the start of World War I.

Modernism meant experimentation, new methods and new techniques in all artistic practices, including music, architecture and painting. In literature, writers like Marcel Proust (1871-1922) with *In Search of Lost Time* and James Joyce (1882-1941) with *Ulysses* were influenced by this new set of ideas. Woolf was also affected by this new spirit of the times, and her work in

To the Lighthouse is considered a masterpiece of modernism.

Modernist writers break with traditional forms of expression and look for new devices that convey human experience in innovative ways. These include the stream of consciousness technique, the concept of time as a subjective experience and the importance of form over content.

The stream of consciousness technique

With this device, the narrative voice reflects the way the human mind flows when it is at work. In the space of just a few moments, a person can think about the present reality, recall a memory and digress on their feelings. Through the stream of consciousness technique, modernist writers experimented on capturing the workings of the mind.

In *To the Lighthouse*, characters are presented through an interior monologue (a narrative device that shows the thoughts inside the characters' minds) using the stream of consciousness technique. This means that their thoughts are not presented in a logical, linear way, but instead shift constantly from one topic to another.

Time as a subjective experience

The innovations introduced by many modernist writers come from a variety of philosophical sources, which were new at the time Woolf wrote *To the Lighthouse*. In particular, Albert Einstein (1879-1955) had recently declared that time was relative, while the philosopher Henry Bergson (1859-1941) claimed that there is a difference between scientific time and the subjective experience of time for each of us.

These ideas influenced the narrative pace of many modernist literary works. For instance, in *To the Lighthouse,* time can stop indefinitely as the characters' feelings are explored. Woolf also played with time by dividing the two days depicted in her novel with a ten-year interlude, which in the book lasts for less than 20 pages.

The importance of form over content

Modernist writers experimented by creating works that focused mainly on the form of the writing and less on the plot. For instance, *To the Lighthouse* pays a great deal of attention to the characters' inner lives. It does so through extreme formal experimentation, including very short or very long sentences and an original use of punctuation (for example, Mrs. Ramsay, Andrew Ramsay and Prue Ramsay's deaths are recounted in brackets).

A SHIFTING NARRATIVE VOICE

The narrative voice in *To the Lighthouse* is characterised by frequent jumps from one character to another. In formal terms, the narrative voice is in the third person. However, this voice belongs to different characters at different moments. The purpose of this experimental device is to allow the reader to enter the minds of the different characters at different times of the book.

"Time Passes", the central part of the book, is the only section where the narrative voice belongs to a narrator who is outside the story.

THE THEMES IN *TO THE LIGHTHOUSE*

Memory and the passage of time

The book as a whole revolves around time and how it changes a family and their lives over the course of a decade. This is related to Woolf's own memories and recollection of her family holidays. Indeed, there are many ways in which Woolf's family is similar to the Ramsays: the family also went on holiday to the Hebrides and Julia Stephen (Virginia's mother) also died prematurely. Thus, it could be argued that *To the Lighthouse* is Woolf's attempt to recall her own childhood memories.

In the book, there are many references to the passage of time. For instance, in the central part, the abandoned house becomes a symbol for the passage of time and loss.

Two characters in particular are especially concerned about time: Mr. and Mrs. Ramsay. On the one hand, Mr. Ramsay is worried that his philosophical work will not endure when he is gone. On the other hand, Mrs. Ramsay is constantly aware of how time goes by and so she aims to make many occasions memorable.

Art and beauty as ways of healing

The inclusion of the young painter Lily Briscoe in the plot allows Woolf to express her own views on the meaning of art. For Lily, finally being able to put her vision to the canvas gives her instant relief. Art and the creation of beauty therefore act as healing agents, in particular when it comes to the restlessness of the mind. Lily is also able to preserve her memories from her first visit to the summer home through her art.

The subjectivity of life and experience

In her novel, Woolf explores how the same event can be experienced differently by different people. She does this mainly through her use of the lighthouse. For James, the lighthouse symbolised an unattainable mystery during his childhood. However, in the third part of the novel, when he approaches the lighthouse by boat, he sees it as a plain and ordinary object of reality. He then moves on to reflect on how the lighthouse can be both ordinary and mysterious, appealing and boring, depending on a person's perspective.

This exploration of subjectivity is enhanced by the shifting perspective of the narrative voice. Woolf uses different narrators in order to show how the same event can be seen differently by different actors in the plot. This gives readers an aggregate view of the actions, as seen subjectively by different characters.

War

The novel is structured around World War I: the first part is set during the pre-war period; during the second part, war breaks out; and the third part corresponds to the postwar period and the effects of the conflict on the people who survived.

During the second part of the novel, the characters' lives in *To the Lighthouse* are significantly changed, and some of them die.

Furthermore, the house falls into disrepair during the war. The family can only come back to it after it has been cleaned. This mirrors the reconstruction efforts after World War I and the population's desire to return to normality.

FURTHER REFLECTION

SOME QUESTIONS TO THINK ABOUT...

- Discuss the importance of war in Woolf's life and work.
- Death is present throughout the book. How do the different characters reflect on it?
- List the remarks made by different characters on gender roles. What does this tell us about Woolf's ideas on feminism?
- "The great revelation perhaps never did come. Instead there were little daily miracles" (p. 142). Consider how this sentence applies to the almost total absence of plot in the book.
- In your opinion, why does Woolf choose to write about the family's deaths using brackets?
- How would the novel be different if Woolf had chosen a traditional narrative voice?
- Make a note of the images or phrases that are repeated in the book (such as Mrs. Ramsay knitting a stocking). What do these repetitions add to the reading of *To the Lighthouse*?

- Discuss Mrs. Ramsay's influence on the different characters. Compare how she influences people before and after her death.

We want to hear from you!
Leave a comment on your online library
and share your favourite books on social media!

FURTHER READING

REFERENCE EDITION

- Woolf, V. (1993) *To the Lighthouse*. London: Longman Group Limited.

REFERENCE STUDIES

- Mondi, M. (2006) "You Find Us Much Changed": The Great War in *To the Lighthouse*. The Delta: Vol. 1: Iss. 1, Article 5. [Online]. [Accessed 17 September 2018]. Available from <http://digitalcommons.iwu.edu/delta/vol1/iss1/5>

- Watkin, C. (2012) Modernism: Narrative point of view in *To the Lighthouse*. [Online]. [Accessed 17 September 2018]. Available from: <https://christopherwatkin.com/2012/06/29/modernism-narrative-point-of-view-in-to-the-lighthouse-modernism-narrative-point-of-view-in-to-the-lighthouse/>

ADDITIONAL SOURCES

- Bell, Q. N. (1972) *Virginia Woolf: A Biography*. London, Hogarth Press.

- Woolf, V. (2003) *A Writer's Diary: Being Extracts from the Diary of Virginia Woolf.* London: Harvest Book.

ADAPTATIONS

- *To the Lighthouse.* (1983) [Film]. Colin Gregg. Dir. UK: British Broadcasting Corporation (BBC).

- *To the Lighthouse.* (2014) [Radio drama]. Linda Marshall Griffiths. Dir. UK: British Broadcasting Corporation (BBC).

MORE FROM BRIGHTSUMMARIES.COM

- Reading guide – *Mrs Dalloway* by Virginia Woolf.

www.brightsummaries.com

Ebook EAN: 9782808012508

Paperback EAN: 9782808012515

Legal Deposit: D/2018/12603/380

Cover: © Primento

Digital conception by Primento, the digital partner of
publishers.